Rethink Yourself

Rethink Yourself

— Victor Ofosu —

RESOURCE *Publications* · Eugene, Oregon

RETHINK YOURSELF

Resource Publications
An Imprint of Wipf and Stock Publishers
199 W. 8th Ave., Suite 3
Eugene, OR 97401

www.wipfandstock.com

PAPERBACK ISBN: 978-1-6667-5484-1
HARDCOVER ISBN: 978-1-6667-5485-8
EBOOK ISBN: 978-1-6667-5486-5

09/28/22

Contents

CONTENTS

Biography

Victor Ofosu (Born May 9th, 1978) is a British author, and equality campaigner. Victor is the author of "The Demise of Arms Control: Non-compliance and the New World Order". He has also published work in local newspapers in the United Kingdom.

Victor's first book is "The Demise of Arms Control: Non-compliance and the New World Order," published in 2020. The book examines the demise of arms control and accesses the devastating nature of a total nuclear war if the world's citizens neglect to hold their respective governments accountable for non-compliance with arms control. The book makes an interesting read as he explains humanity's dangers today.

In August 2010, Victor Ofosu published a documentary, "The Effects of Globalisation on Ghana." This documentary, which was welcomed in the African community, identified the impact of corruption in Ghana. The documentary demonstrates that corruption and greed amongst state actors have directly contributed to its lack of development. The documentary asserts that globalisation has directly impacted Ghana's political and economic development; the adverse effects of globalisation have increased dependency on Western nations.

Victor graduated from Stamford High School in June 1997. After graduation, he moved to London, where he spent six years on London's streets, trying to survive. Victor experienced a difficult life in London. His friend Kwame Sasu Weradu was arrested and subsequently died in police custody. He describes this loss as the turning point in his life. Since then, Victor has attained a Diploma in Business and a Bachelor of Science in International Politics at London South Bank University. He also holds a Master's Degree in Arms Control and International Security from Kings College University in London.

Victor has worked as a journalist, a political activist, an editor, and an event organiser. He has also travelled across Europe, speaking on equality and African development. He has also worked as a Public Relations Manager. He is a businessman and a humanitarian who believes that all men are equal. He is also passionate about arms control. Victor's objective is to see a world where issues dividing society, such as race and gender, are eradicated. A world in which the populace holds the government and interest groups accountable for their actions.

Foreword

T HE PURPOSE OF THIS book is to assist you with understanding the world. The book also seeks to create awareness of the numerous issues afflicting our planet. The book is set to explain your relationship with the earth and with others. It provides an understanding of yourself and provokes the means to achieve your dreams and desires. It attempts to eliminate fears of ourselves, our society and fear generated through embracing social norms. With this book, you will be able to attain happiness and freedom. Understanding your surrounding and the world you live in is paramount in achieving your dreams. Therefore, eliminating any forms of trepidation that may affect your conscious and unconscious mind is vital. For example, if you desire happiness or wealth, getting rid of fear will raise the conviction that there is no limit to what you can achieve as a person. Without fear and understanding of yourself and society, you pose to achieve freedom, happiness, wealth, and self-awareness.

I was once approached by a man who mentioned that he was poor and needed some financial support. He further explained that in the past, he was a wealthy man. He had a family, cars and two houses. However, without warning, he has lost all his possessions. He asks if I can assist him in returning his riches. I observed the man was in poor health. He was also stressed from not being able to cater for his family. I felt emotional about his predicament and replied that I was happy to assist him. However, I could not return his wealth; in my view, attaining wealth is subject to him believing in himself and not in my ability. I insist that my knowledge is centred on my belief that I have the power to help people, and this power was disposed of through the supreme being. As we were near a busy market, I purchased a water bottle and prayed. In my prayer, I requested health and knowledge for the man; I also prayed that he would discover his true purpose, as self-discovery was important toward his financial recovery. After my prayer, I ask the man to pray whilst praying. After I had concluded my activities, I gave £10 with the following instruction. He was not to spend the money. I ask him to return home, pray again before bed, and place the money under his pillow for seven days. He asks, "but what would I eat tonight?" On his way home, I said a woman would appear, and she would offer him the means to buy food for his family. You came to be because you believe I can assist you. I have also mentioned that the first course of action is for you to believe in yourself. If you think that I can help you in your recovery, then do as I have instructed. I left this man, and a year later, he contacted me. He was better, and he was in good health. He mentioned that he is free from poverty, but he is not rich. However, he has a new business and wanted to offer me a gift. I replied that my gift was in his recovery, and thus I wasn't interested in money or any article. The story's moral is that one can oppose failure by believing in oneself.

I am pertinacious in my disposition when I argue that we have lost focus on our true being. We are all seeking wealth to our detriment. We seek wealth first before health and knowledge. With health as our focus, one can have life. And with knowledge, you will be free from mental slavery, from the social contract that imposes unfair and unrealistic rules on your development as a person, free from oppression and repression. With this knowledge, you will be able to conquer failure. Indeed, money is essential as it helps in fulfilling some pleasures. It is also a practical means to one's survival. However, in its abundance, it becomes evil. The possessor of such wealth will seek more wealth to the detriment of the welfare of society and others. With money, you achieve happiness through material possessions. However, these possessions cannot offer your soul true happiness generated from performing charities or attaining spiritual well-being. It is an infallible truth that one can command wealth through meditation, visualisation, committing to speaking the truth, self-realisation and a positive relation with others and nature. Such a person with nature will observe that nature works in their interest. Yet, it is erroneous to believe that material possession will bring them contentment and happiness. Happiness can only be attained in the joy of living. The joy of living can be achieved through committing to positive actions towards society and others. However, having passion is chief to a living and will also provide fulfilment in the joy of living. It is vital that you should seek the joy of living through health and knowledge before seeking material possessions.

Acknowledgements

I DEDICATE THIS BOOK, THE knowledge in each department to the universe and humanity. I would like to recognise the universe for the knowledge instructed to me, to interpret to humanity. I would like to give thanks to my children Sofia and Afua. I would also like to recognise my wife, Suvi Marija, for her patience and support. She was instrumental in the book's composition and motivating and encouraging. Her love and understanding have brought together the family. I want to acknowledge my designer Jenny Katharina Maus; her input and contribution have made the book possible. She is solely responsible for the images and illustrations in this book. Jenny has shown that she believes in my ideas. She was committed to capturing my vision in her pictures and drawings. I would like to thank my cousin David Ofori-Atta. David has always been my bigger brother. He has been my mentor for the past 20 years. David always believed in me and was determined to ensure that I achieved greatness.

Introduction

COVID-19 HAS REDUCED THE quality of life across all spectrums of British society. However, it is understood that the impact is not uniformly felt. The impact depends on the individual's location in the country. Be as it may, Covid-19 is negatively affecting life and taking life. Covid-19 continues to increase levels of trepidation in the country and has increased social and economic inequalities in the United Kingdom and many countries across the globe. The negative outcome of COVID-19 presents a disadvantage for various societies across the globe. It creates a burden on economic and social development growth. Community and community action has become more relevant at this time.

The author's observation of the current situation in the U.K. and across the world suggests the need for further integration.

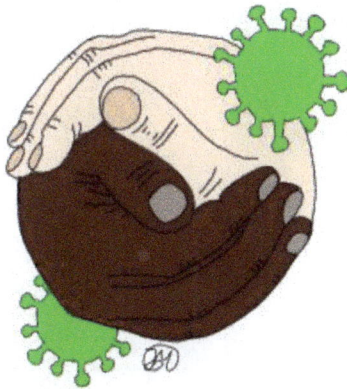

The collection of poems is a lamentation of the current state of the world. It offers an emotional understanding of the suffering faced by the world's population. Yet, as the author resides in the United Kingdom, his observation concerns issues, and situations in the country manifest in his writing. His writing illustrates how the people in Britain feel about the current pandemic and the socio-economic decline of the country. The poems are written in thirty-eight chapters, and they are an illustration of how the population feels. The book addresses issues concerning the individual and health, wealth, spirituality, and global struggles. The author hopes the poems will also bring light to people's lives. Therefore, he disperses a message of confidence and courage to the reader. The poems are not designed and intended as a solution to the current issues facing the world's population, but they create awareness and attempt to allow individuals to understand these issues by understanding themselves and their contribution to society. The poems generate the need for the individual to accept change by changing their lifestyle and how they interact with society. The author is passionate about improving human conditions; as such, he calls for the need for humanity to improve its relationship with the planet. The author also calls for humans to strengthen relationships and thus ensure a better future.

Chapter 1

Britain Can Make It

COVID-19 HAS TAKEN HOLD on Britain; There is a smell of death, a rotting smell of decay mingling with fear across the country. Britain came to a halt. Death crippled our lives; death crippled our economy; death changed the face of Britain, but Britain made it. But Britain can make it.

The dusk deepened; a gloomy dark cloud covered Britain with a mist spreading across the country. The dark cloud cast a shadow of death into our lives. Our supermarkets were left with crumbs; the fear of starvation developed into waves of tsunamis sweeping across Britain, yet Britain can make it.

The battle for Britain has begun. The fight to save our burdened National Health Service has begun. It has been a quiet two years. COVID invaded our homes and invaded our country; it killed and destroyed. COVID, cancer that supersedes all cancers begun a battle against humanity. The disease sent from hell to unleash catastrophic devastation on humanity unleashed its weapon to destroy Britain. Britain can make it. Britain knows nothing but its need to survive; therefore, Britain can make it.

Deaths across the country have increased, sorrow and fears continue to burden our country. The media continues to propagate survival and defence against COVID. The media have infiltrated our hearts, minds, and souls. The media has unleashed an avalanche of ice, extinguishing the hot laver of fear which has settled in our minds. Britain can make it.

Yes, Britain can make it; the Brits are fighting the invisible enemy, fighting to save a life, we will survive again. We survived the horrific Nazi bombings and won the battle for Britain, and today, we shall win the battle against COVID. Britain can make it. The people's army of nurses and doctors have battled the unthinkable; they have laid down their lives to save Britain. Such courage and actions show Britain's strength, showing that Britain can win the battle. Britain can make it.

The nurses, the doctors, the hospital cleaners, the security officers, the police, the bus driver, the taxi driver and the London ambulance servicemen and women are fighting the battle against COVID-19. The strength of each frontline worker is the sound of the crashing thunder. Many will fall to COVID, but the brave fighting to save Britain will throw themselves into the jaws of death. Britain can make it.

Britain is under siege again and again; COVID attempts to win the battle. The invisible enemy has the strength of a million tigers'; it has sucked its teeth into the old, tearing into the flesh of the vulnerable. The sirens are wailing, Britain is on the street again, fighting to survive. The battle with the invisible enemy will repeat itself. The music of death may strike every home, but Britain will not give up; Britain can make it.

Britain is prepared to defeat this evil; we shall defeat this evil. Britain can make it. Britain fights for the day the first siren will be waled for the end of COVID 19. And yes, the sirens will be heard. Britain can make it; The battle for Britain shall be won. Soon Britain will raise its head to shake off death's scythe. COVID will no longer reap the soul of its population; Britain will finally be free. Britain can make it.

—— Chapter 2 ——

Save the Orphans

J UST IMAGINE THE AMOUNT of food we waste each day. Imagine the amount of water we waste each day; imagine a child travelling miles in search of water; imagine the pain and plight of this child; just imagine. Imagine the number of children faced with starvation, fathers and mothers who died from COVID-19, leaving behind children without a future. Imagine the struggle of the orphan displaced and in search of food. Just imagine a child of 3 years old gathering food from the dumps of the rich man. We are consumed with greed, and our sense of humanity has been eroded. The jagged edges of covid have unleashed its holocaust; the modern-day Auschwitz has revealed itself. Death has crippled our lives; covid has crippled families. Every newborn without a family will suffer; just imagine their pain. Just imagine how covid has enslaved our society. Just imagine the sorrow felt by the orphan, just imagine. This is the time we must come together to save the children. Just imagine what will happen if we ignore the plight of the orphan.

—— Chapter 3 ——

Who Are They?

"WHO ARE THEY?" COULD it be the state whose ambition is focused on subjecting its population to torture? Could it be the state, the system whose rationale is to suppress and rule the masses? Perhaps, it is the system drawn and shaped to preserve the elite's economic significance. "Who are they"? Are they the police, the army, legally responsible for providing the apparatus to rule humanity? Are they the individuals accountable for our legal system, lawmakers, and politicians? Could it possibly be the politicians who indulge themselves in the pleasure of corruption? Are they the individual subjecting our minds to the word freedom while repressing our souls with policies to restrain our freedom? "Who are they"? Are they our leaders subject the masses to stress and eradicate human dignity? Our leaders, whose greed has led many to their mercy, is it their brutal and barbaric army, the men and women of the force who overlook the need to protect the population from the extreme ideologies approved by their commander? Are they the elite whose army murders and destroys society to preserve and maintain power? Are they the individuals liable for the murders of the men and women of our armed forces?

"Who are they"? They are those responsible for the tears in a mother's eye. Those accountable for the hunger and deaths of many children, preaching equality, practice an ideology of divide and rule. Those who encourage the notions of unequal distribution of wealth and alienation are the multinationals, liable for the destruction of our planet. They are the individual who fosters a utopian society, which destroys Mother Nature's beauty. Are they the NATO, the United Nations, whose manifesto entails protecting the world population? Is it the United Nations, a club of wealthy nations whose aim to regulate world resources, has prompted wars and revolutions? "Who are they"? Could it perchance be the preacher, the churches, the Pope, and the educational institutions who have led the masses into a state of ignorance? They are those who preach peace but practise a policy of hate. Are they the individuals blinded by material wealth and who live a life of hatred, exploitation, and envy? "Who are they"?

Chapter 4

Life

WITH EACH YEAR, YOUR spirit evolves further beyond the constraint of Covid. With perseverance, you have survived COVID-19's massacre. You strive to survive will present you with long life and blessings.

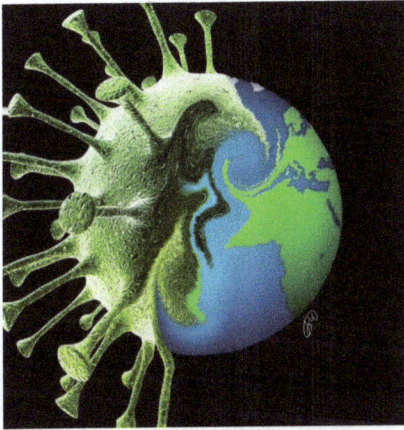

Life today gives you much strength, and on this very day, you rise above your enemy covid, 19—the only enemy of humanity to exert pain and anguish on humankind. The stars wish you happiness and the best of life is on offer. Your deepest dreams and wishes will come to pass, and you will survive the killer covid. Fear not; be proud; life without happiness is not worth living. Today, your wisdom will perceive that contentment lies not in material possession but the joy of life; you will shine as you were born to shine.

— Chapter 5 —

Chosen Angel

A YEAR OF DEATH, ILLNESS, disasters, and a lack of meaning to the word life. The disaster cripples the mind to believe happiness and love can only exist in the afterlife. The wondering soul caught up in the tangle of the underworld, how I wonder why life could have led me into the belly of the beast.

The dreams of a better future: a life of prosperity smashed by envy and jealousy, a year of sorrow and despair. Despite this anguish, I woke up to a voice of an angel, the voice of harmony, tranquillity, and peace sparking life in my soul and heart. It was clear my soul was at rest. My mind gallops and restlessly investigates the reason for my happiness and freedom. Oh, how clear can it be, how obvious can it be that you are the angel from the heavens? Chosen to lead me towards righteousness, in your image, I am blinded by your beauty, and in the physical, my mind submits to your humble requests. Indeed, you are my guardian angel and angel among all angels.

—————— Chapter 6 ——————

Grant Me Your Love

M Y HEART BEATS TO the sound of your love. Your love flows through my heart as your love is the stream of life. Life without you is like shattered glasses without a purpose. You are the purpose for my creation and the goal of my dreams. How many times have I said I love you, and how many times should I explain the size of the hole in my heart? Your love candles my heart like the flame of a candle. A small flame amongst many, but with the strength to burn a hole in my heart. Your love is the hope by which I live. Your love sings the truth, and the truth of your heart shall remain in the sight of the angels.

Oh, my humble Queen, my words are meaningless in expressing the joy you bring to my heart. You are sweet to my flavour, and your beauty makes every night different from the other. Oh, my dearest one, your lips are as sweet and soft as chocolate from the finest trees. The love in your eye sparkles brighter than the stars. Your love candles my heart like the flame of the candle. Why should I or would I forget or neglect such love yet to be discovered by man? Yet my heart is unable to discover the intensity of your love.

My first laugh in the morning is through the passion of your eyes. My last laugh shall be the sweetness of your love. Could it be madness or the conflict within the boundaries of my heart that has set my heart at blaze? I seek no further but for the purity of your love; oh, my love, grant me your love, as you may grant a man his soul. And I shall sing songs of your love in life and thereafter.

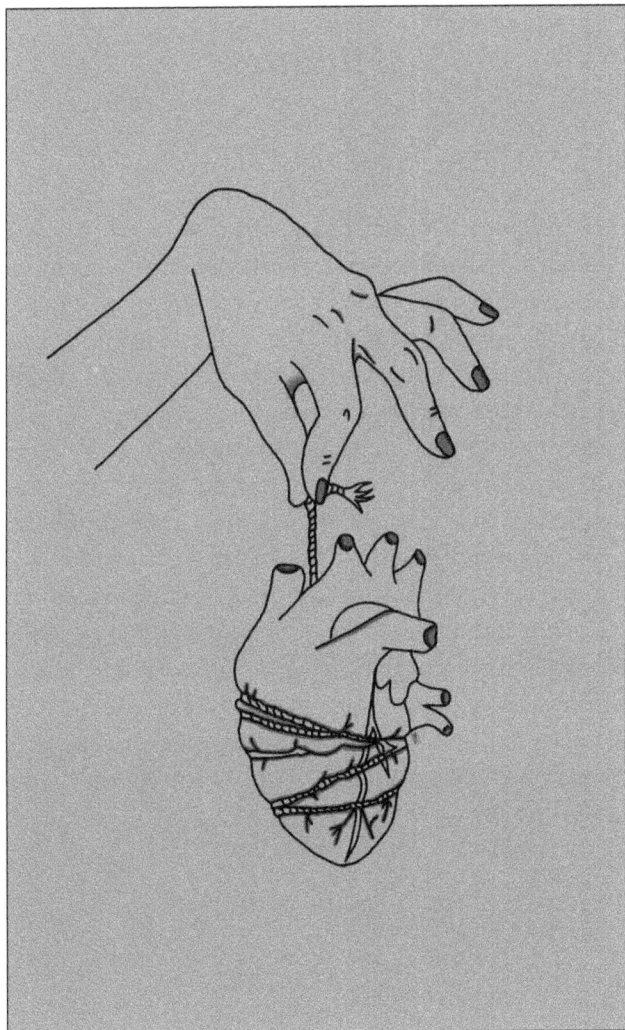

Chapter 7

Hidden

T HE MOST DIFFICULT FEELING to pursue in life is love. Love presents tremendous pain, which can lead a person to his grave. Could it be imagination or reality of the true meaning of love? The subjective feeling leads a man or woman to lose his soul. Love has no arms but can touch you in ways you cannot see. Sometimes, those we love are consumed by themselves and are interested in objects and activities they pursue.

The heart of a dying man or woman, filled with love and passion for his love, disappears as he feels alone in the wilderness. Oh, what a feeling so strong to make a man or woman engage in a so-called pleasure killing. To love or to hate, to hate or to live in the shadow of love, or to avoid the unexpected pain called love. Yet, one's mind believes in the purity of true love. In a state of confusion, one may pursue happiness in others or live in the shadows of the unimaginable. Betrayed by those he feels for, and hope could understand him. A lonely soul yet with a heart of a thousand angels.

Chapter 8

The London Irony

TODAY I FIND MYSELF sitting at Waterloo station contemplating where this country is heading while dreading the final days of our lives. Today, I feel the entire world is against me, but my soul prays for change. Today, they starve the poor for their self-interest.

Today, people will struggle just to survive. The people in politics claim the rights of the people to assist the poor, but we are ignored, beaten, or murdered for standing up for our basic human rights. Is it my purpose to anchor change? An anchor of change, I will cry, talk, chat, and post until I draw my last breath. Yet could this be a dream? Could this be a dream that may never manifest? I am consumed by shame; my lack of bravery and confidence affects my mind. My mind is scared of itself. Scared to speak and scared to realise its truth. The truth sits within itself whiles the struggle within my mind battles with itself. Today, the fight for justice rests in my mind. Scared of my own shadow, I fight the unspeakable battle. Today, I see heroes around me in the same battle. A battle not in the physical and a battle that tears into your mind. A struggle for justice that is in vain.

Chapter 9

I am who I am

I am back again,

I was here with you last year when you were all alone,

The year of sorrow and sadness is over.

I bring life, light, and a new sense of worth.

I made you smile after months of stress and unhappiness.

I am the season of grace, presents and the light towards
a new beginning.

I am the joy around you and the reason for your happiness.

I am the season of forgiveness and the cause of purity.

The time to love and the time to give, I am the pride of the year,

Yes, I am who I am

Chapter 10

Human Destiny

O UR MAD AND GLOOMY civilisation lacks respect for humanity, revealing nothing less than a disintegrating civilisation. Universally, humanity can recognise the beauty of nature. Yet we create our miseries as we attempt to accomplish the much-envied utopian society that deforms nature's beauty. Instead of bathing in nature's light, we lose ourselves in the hell of this self-manifested utopia. Nature is the most magnificent creation, producing a place for any man or woman to coexist peacefully. Today, the dignity of humanity represents the need for one individual to oppress the other for self-satisfaction without recognising the destruction caused to nature.

This action is facilitated by crooks, dictators, and murderers who call themselves our leaders. The idea or concept of human rights has become an unpleasant mirage in the desert. We crave no less than a drop of water that frees our souls from the terror imposed by our regimes. Humans are divided, excluded, and alienated by their colours, cultures, and traditions. Many are perceived as subhuman beings based on their individualised beliefs or colours. We are imprisoned by our minds, corrupted by greed and lack of self-respect.

Humans observe self-confidence in material assets and refuse to recognise nature's purity and beauty. The universal man can exist by spreading our cultures and ideas. The true beauty of our planet lies in the purity of our hearts. The strength we seek for change lies within each person. Our planet should not be sold to private interests but should be cherished and enjoyed by all.

Chapter 11

Freedom

E VER SINCE THE DAWN of man, the weak have struggled to rise against those who wish to enslave them. The strike of lighting and the row of thunder is yet to set him free from oppression. Humanities' quest for material wealth has blinded our sight to the true nature of our current global democracy. Embedded within our free democracy is the strength of economic slavery. Within this process, the oppressor shows his courage through undisclosed slavery. The cries of the oppressed are heard through their prayers and the blood which pours out of their cries. Those who possess the courage to stand against the system are murdered, but new ones replace the dead. Slavery today knows no race or gender but the need to deprive all men of their human rights. It perpetuates the perception of a free world of economic trade and freedom of speech. But in fact, we live in nothing less than a controlled state. Freedom is not far, as the sun is from the moon. Freedom can be achieved, just like clearing cobwebs full of spiders. The oppressor has the strength of machines that can move rocks. But the enslaved, in their numbers, can move the oppressor with the passion and courage of their heart. A world free of misery is possible, but are we ready to do away with material wealth blinding our view of the true nature of our world? Make a stand, as the change you create today may better the youth tomorrow.

Chapter 12

Courage

If you believe in yourself, you will achieve.

Once there is a light, there is always a chance.

Gather your courage and overcome your struggles.

If you are let down, find the courage to move on.

Look within yourself and find that positive feeling,

lead yourself from the darkness and find true happiness.

You thought you would never be happy,

Look up in the sky, and you will find your star is shining,

free your mind and soul.

You are an angel, be strong and look out for opportunities ahead.

Today could be the day your life changes for the better.

Chapter 13

Wondering Soul

The wondering heart is less significant than your soul.

The hate we project cripples our soul

The revenge we seek may satisfy the mind,

but vengeance leaves the soul impure and wounded.

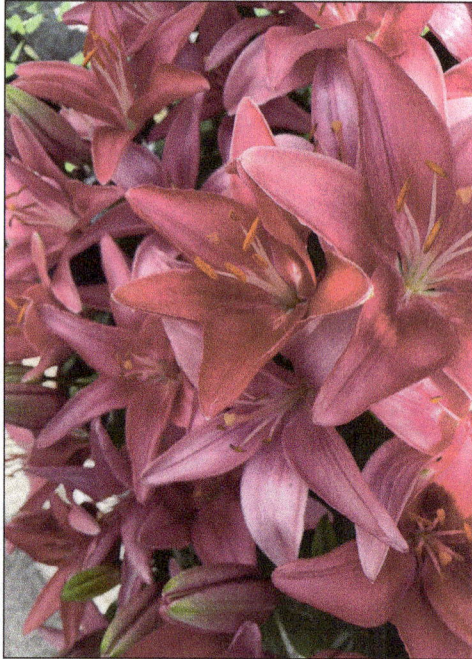

Free your soul from the cruelty of your mind and embrace
the gifts which follow forgiveness.

Your future is blessed as your heart is as pure as gold.

Seek no revenge, and the soul will free itself of your pain.

The end of your struggles is near,

separating your soul from the pleasures of revenge.

Embrace the light which seeks to bring you glory.

Chapter 14

True Love, Master of my Heart

On this day, I feel the best of your love

In my heart and mind,

I will love you until all love freezes like the ice on the Pole.

You are as beautiful as the goddess of love.

The angel sings the praise of your beauty,

As no man with an eye can resist your charm and beauty,

Your lips are the thread of my life.

Indeed, I will be a fool to your love on this very day and forever.

As your love will cure the wound in my heart, oh, my dearest
loves, to my heart, you are the only master in this world.

TRUE LOVE, MASTER OF MY HEART

The moon lights the oasis by night, and your love lights
my heart by day.

The shine of the sun on your beauty makes me lose my senses,

My heart goes to you, the love of my heart,

Who is as pure as the green pastures.

Make no man can take you away from me, as my heart
will bleed to death.

You are all I love, my pride and joy and all I will ever need.

Chapter 15

Your New Beginning

You may feel you failed,

you may feel it is all over,

but this is only the beginning.

Fear not, for your time is near,

have faith in yourself.

Listen to your inner self and ignore negativity,

for the path to your future has just been written.

Draw yourself out of the darkness,

stir yourself into the light.

For the sun and the stars are shining on you,

you are your dream, and your dream will come true.

Chapter 16

Maintain Your Confidence

I was born confident, but yesterday I lost my confidence.

Today I have courage; tomorrow,

I will gain and maintain my confidence.

I will hold my head high and have the confidence
to achieve my goals.

People wish to discourage me because I have confidence.

But I will maintain my confidence as the light assures
it will stay with me.

Today I remember I am confident; tomorrow,

I will encourage others to be confident.

The sun shines on me because I have confidence,

and I will live the rest of my day with confidence.

Chapter 17

Oh, Mother Earth

Oh, mother earth, how I adore you.

Oh, mother earth, thanks for the life you have given us.

The food you generate and the oxygen you breathe on us.

Oh, mother earth, thanks for your love and attention.

What can one ask or do to protect you?

Forgive us for our ignorance and show us how to
protect you from men's jaws.

Man's greed has led to the distraction of your beauty.

Man's greed has marked a scar on your beauty.

Oh, mother earth, forgive a man for his crimes against
your humble existence.

Oh, mother earth, words cannot explain my love and
how grateful I am for the life you create.

—— Chapter 18 ——

Racist Free World

M OST COUNTRIES PRIDE THEMSELVES on being committed to Human Rights. They are the foundations on which we build a healthy, civilised nation. However, racism is still a big issue today, and we can see that racism causes division, fear and violence, and harmful ideas that fascism feeds and thrives on. The system in which we live divides people. As the gap between rich and poor grows, people feel dispossessed, angry, and insecure. The basis of this system is competition, causing division not only within races but also within social classes. Most people at the bottom of this social ladder today are people of colour.

Since the abolition of slavery in the 1820s, people of colour have been denied advancement; the segment of society has been deprived of the knowledge and opportunities needed to break the cycle of poverty and violence, inevitably leading to problems with criminal and antisocial behaviour. Even today, people forget that racism is a product of ignorance, fear of the unknown and fear of different things. Some people are blinded by that fear and resort to violence. It is sad that people still get killed because of the colour of their skin. Race division will always lead to individualism, selfishness, hatred and sometimes even war. It is time for us to learn from our past and make changes for the future. We need to look at ourselves, then at each other and be able to see past the physical and cultural differences. We must be aware of each other as humans, each responsible for their actions and sharing this planet. It is not about skin colour but about who we are. Humans thrive by communicating with each other and their surroundings.

Helping each other will benefit society and reduce hatred and division. Life is a cycle, and within this cycle, we all have our roles to play, and it is by being united that we will bring progress to our society. We must stand against fear and injustice. Let us unite in our mission to eradicate racism. Let us save our World!

—— Chapter 19 ——

The Forgotten

D UE TO THE POPULATION increase, unemployment and homelessness are unaddressed issues. Homelessness is not a choice. The lack of housing has been quoted as a reason for homelessness, but there are nearly a million empty houses. So, the problem is a governmental lack of adequate policy. There are numerous causes of homelessness, including but not restricted to the breakdown of the family system, drug and alcohol addiction, abuse of the individual, unemployment, lack of education and mental health problems. There is also a problem with easy access to help centres. Many homeless people are those living on the margins of our society. Those who have been in the social services' care and those released from either prison or mental health institutions, ex-servicemen and women form a substantial proportion of the homeless, generally because very few aftercare services are available for service personnel who suffer the after-effects of being in a war zone. Many people see a family member with mental health issues as something to be ashamed of, especially in some ethnic minority communities. It is never spoken about, kept behind closed doors, so the available help is never sorted out. This, in turn, means the problems are left unaddressed.

Many reasons for homelessness lead to social isolation, which only exacerbates the problems. What is needed is a more open-door approach from the government to solve these problems. Society can do a great deal to address the problem; by not looking the other way, we can lead a hand in solving the problem. We need, as a society, to engage with the homeless, to stretch out the hand of friendship, even if it's something as simple as spending 5 minutes talking to a homeless person. You would be surprised how much difference that would make to the homeless person and yourself. We individuals make up the society; we need to reconnect with each other and realise that the material goods we are searching for make us divisive and inhuman.

– Chapter 20 –

The Future

T HE FUTURE PRESENTS US with severe uncertainty. Humans have developed too fast in the wrong way heading in the wrong direction. Humans today believe we have accomplished the impossible, but in reality, we are destroying ourselves and our whole existence. The definition of development presents the notion that we expropriate, live, and die, understanding that we are leaving behind what is needed for the youth to develop. Nevertheless, development today is the wrong way forward for a productive future for the youth.

Today we fight amongst ourselves for our own material needs, forgetting to preserve nature for the future. We must understand that nature and land are for the usage of all men, women, children and most importantly, animals. Sadly, our greed has created an impossible utopian society that is the beginning and the end of our existence. We forget humans, just like the forest and animals have significance in future. Our various governments today preach the need to preserve nature, yet; on the other hand, they are all too eager to sign agreements with corporations involving the destruction of our forests. They wage unnecessary war and, in the course, kill animals and destroy our beautiful nature. I dreamed of a day when humans will be ready to forgo all their desires, leading to our destruction.

I see a future where water and food would be the cause of major wars, a future where our destruction of nature would lead to suffering and incurable diseases, and a future where man will fight against the rebellion of nature, manifesting itself in different forms.

I see a future when humans wish they could go back in time and undo their mistakes. However, it is not too late for man to develop the right way and put the future on the right course. I pray that all understand the need to preserve our beautiful planet by respecting ourselves, animals, and, most importantly, the forest. We should only use what is needed and not overproduce for our ambitions. The solution to a better future is government policy and living life responsibly. Also, through education and development, we still have a chance for future survival. I warn all men and women that it is time to make the right decision to better the future.

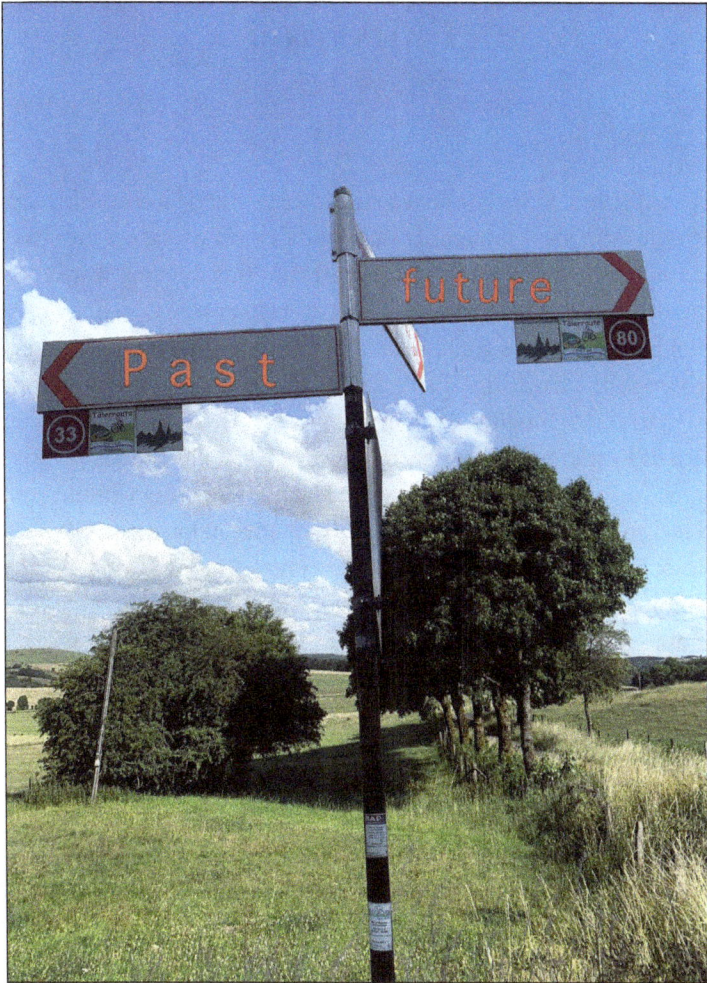

– Chapter 21 –

I Miss You

I T IS HARD TO say goodbye to those we love and have lost through the struggle. I remember our good time as we sat on the street corner contemplating how to progress in this unequal world. We made plans not only to develop but to help ensure equality. I cannot believe you are gone. Also, to my friends who did not make it through the hardship of street life, I promise to maintain our vision to create equality. Although you are gone, I know and feel you are still with me. Kwame, sorry I never said all I had to say because now you are gone. I never imagined I would be living without you. I feel you here with me, which keeps me alive in my quest. We both took life for granted, but I hope you know I always cared. All the summers we spent together felt you would forever be here. But now, my sleepless night makes me feel all is lost. But in my heart, I will always carry you and initiate your dreams.

Kwame, you were a wild young man blessed with the foul lesson of this unfair society. We both mess with the wrong crowd and learn our lesson. We spent days stressing about life and praying about how to get out of the streets. We spent time hurting our kind, but Kwame, now I see the bigger picture. I have forgotten the criminal ways; now, it is about educating the youth about our struggles. It was always a hustle on the street going through society's ills. Sometimes, when we had the police running after us, it felt like equality was a counterfeit. They said all men were equal, but we were treated as different species when we got stopped. Through our struggles, we took advantage of the hard life we were born into. The establishment never valued us, but we always knew our existence was priceless. Throughout our mission, the devil had plans to take you away from me. We always felt we could not trust the government, and through the process, the police took you away. A few years after your death, the young men today are killing each other, which was not the case with us. Sadly, the institution whose responsibility it is to protect us took your life. Before your arrest, I waited for your return to commence our plans for change. But the following day, I was informed you were gone. I never had the chance to say goodbye. For the love of money, we were dragged down into negativity; only if we had education and liberty would this world have been a better place for us. Kwabena has never been the same since you have gone, but he has the family he always wanted today. Kwame, we are now doing just fine.

Chapter 22

The Youth and The Future

T HE MOST SERIOUS THREAT to Great Britain is not terrorism or state security but handling our internal economic affairs. Today our country is confronted with an economic affliction of significant proportion. I stress the point that the state of the British economy is deteriorating. Our main problem accumulating to this issue is that our parents have been too selfish. Sadly, this generation of youth will one day be responsible for paying the bills left by our parents. Although this is the case, we, the people, have a choice. To solve the problem, we require spending discipline. By this, I mean the government and the people need to stop spending money they do not have.

The solution should take effect on both the social and governmental levels. The process requires a partnership between the masses and the government, and a partnership requires more savings and less credit usage. The problem we face today results from housing crises and issues left to spill over from the First and Second World Wars. Our high borrowing, fraud, and financial market uncertainty can also be blamed for these crises.

Today in 2021, our economy is suffering and bleeding from the inside, and now a garrotte will not help us; we need to beat the economic crisis. We cannot simply cut and paste using foreign financial templates. It is in our best interest to address the issue as it suits the British people.

We, the people, need to call our government to implement a measure to attend to this illness to better the future. We need more robust economic growth, which may depend on lower inflation.

To acquire low inflation, we need more interest in saving and less interest in the stock market. I see that the effect of a permanent arms economy which moves our attention from addressing social issues to the production of arms, is also to blame for our problem. On this issue, our government invests more in arms production to protect our country.

Nevertheless, they wage war on countries such as Iraq to make money from arms sales. For me, investing in our manufacturing industries and small businesses will be the right solution. I believe this solution will increase employment, contributing to saving to secure the future. However, I argue that the state of our economy is also a result of short-term measures implemented by our governments. Our leaders gave us the impression that we could spend and borrow at will. As a result, we were mortgaging the future of our youth, leaving them with the responsibility to pay for our own mistakes. The current measures implemented by our government will only lead to high taxation and extended deficits. I, at this moment, stress the need for severe measures to be implemented for the future leaders of our country to manage our economy. If these measures are not implemented, future leaders will have less quality of life than our current leaders have enjoyed. Our country needs to export more and import less to control our trade deficit. This solution, in the long run, will manage our debt. I say this because I foresee a future where our governance will be unaffordable. Tomas Jefferson argues that it is immoral to leave the future generation with debt during his time. My fellow citizens, we are the future and the generation affected by the current economic mismanagement. We must act now to secure a better future. We must not simply go according to what is presented by our leaders; we need to take effective action for a better tomorrow.

Chapter 23

Rethinking Our future

I T WAS LATE AFTERNOON in March 2020; Britain was again pre-
paring for the night. There is a gloomy and miserable feeling in
the night—most of Britain's anxiously awaiting the prime minister's
announcement. COVID-19 has taken hold of the country; there is
an expectation that the government will rescue England from the
invisible enemy. The destructive arms of COVID-19 have reduced
Britain to a ghost country. The fear and devastation impact of
COVID can be seen and felt around us. We cannot defeat COVID
with nuclear weapons, nor can it be shot with an AK 47; it cannot
be touched. COVID is the invisible enemy. Our weapons have been
rendered useless against the striking force of COVID-19.

There is a fear of death in every household and a fear of dis-
ease carriers; COVID-19 has divided families and turned friends
into enemies. It has transformed Britain into a police state. A
once divided society has further deteriorated, and the mistrust
in society has increased as each attempt to survive the great evil
that has befallen humanity. For the first time, Britain is going
into lockdown. Those left on Britain's streets are rushing home;
darkness has fallen on England.

A gloomy dark cloud covers Britain with a mist that appears to be spreading across the city. The dark cloud has cast a shadow of death into our lives. The television announces the increase in deaths across the country; sorrow and fears continue to burden our country and propagate fear into our hearts and minds. The media have infiltrated our hearts, minds, and souls. The media has unleashed hot lava of fear deep into our minds and souls, and its destruction is as lethal as COVID-19. They announce that the number of deaths is soaring, and our fears are escalating. We feel restless, aware that this is an unpleasant way to live our life and an unpleasant way to exist.

The last two years have shown that there are forces beyond our control, demonstrating the need for humanity to integrate to preserve our nation. Here, the question of freedom develops in the individuals' minds, which leads to the understanding that the impact of this phenomenon (COVID-19) has changed the course of human history. The question of freedom or its lack has become an integral part of our lives today. The right to acquire our freedom through acquiring knowledge can exist as an internal and external component of the individual. Knowledge and freedom become the primary concept of our existence.

Covid-19, in our present time, has limited the internal and external existence of freedom; as an evil entity, it limits our freedom and replaces freedom with fear. Through Covid, the will and freedom of each Britain belong to the government and the entities responsible for managing humanity. Managing our immediate future is warranted, allowing eradicating the fear that has settled in our hearts and minds. The devastating impact of Covid-19 requires addressing; humanity must implement direct action to reduce the rising number of deaths and sorrows being suffered by humankind. The action will stem from our passions, talents, and endeavours to obtain our freedoms from those who control our existence. The goal can be achieved through the development of the universal aim. The universal aim will be achieved through patriotism, morality, and freedom. These are the aim that can effect change and reduce the frustration that has weakened the soul of our nation. These virtues can direct actions dedicated to the attainment of our freedom. The concept of freedom does not permeate a revolution but recognises the internal (soul and spirit) that we lost through our actions. External freedom concerns recognising a lack of reason in our actions, which affects an entire society or nation. Our desire for freedom from Covid-19 is limited. Whilst one may understand the importance of the universal aim, personal limitation and external influence can affect their ability to attain freedom.

During the last two lockdowns in England, we have systematically moved from a divided society to embracing each other. Individualism has become a thing of the past, or though it can be traced in our societies. Nevertheless, families stand together in the battle against Covid. The experience should be preserved as it will assist in the creation of a better future for Britain. The future may acknowledge the individual's rights, but individualism as the dominant thinking could be reduced; here, the achievement of the individual will be observed through the achievement of the state.

Individualism is a subjective concept that affects our ability to reason, clouding our judgement and restricting rationality in our thinking. Instead of indulging in our passions, the universal aim should take precedence. Our passion which translates into our satisfaction from our selfish desires are forces that require eradicating. Before the prevalence of Covid, individuals obtained power from their selfish desires, limiting their ability to observe the full effect of nature's laws, social norms, values, and morality. The law, social norms, values, and morality are better for our nation. Our selfishness limited our ability to understand and observe the law of nature. However, we turn to developing and forging a relationship with artificial objects produced by man. Today, in the presence of covid, selfishness and the passions attached to artificial articles are causation for the human drama that has activated violence on an unprecedented scale around the world. Issues manifesting through lack of reason and a limitation in the rationale in human thinking have been exhibited in countless wars, starvation, and genocides worldwide. The link between reason, rationality in thinking, good intention, and good action, which is embedded in the soul and spirit of humankind, has been replaced by the flourishing of wickedness and a decline in morals. It is hoped that experiences gained from Covid would again establish the importance of morality and freedom in the populace's hearts. Today, the British population battle for every opportunity to live another day. We have embraced the notion that death is with us to stay, and anyone could be a victim. There is also the realisation of human life's importance, a belief that has long been replaced by money, greed, and self-gratification. The decline and fall of our values, freedom and morality are not the works of nature but an issue resulting from man's will.

Nature is outraged by our behaviour. We have lost the spirit of goodness and our devotion to each other. In its place, we replaced the former with aggression and consumption of consumer products. Covid has printed a picture of horror in our present-day and the future; this horror affects all men and women. The picture printed by the impact of covid affects the mode of production, a factor contributing to our society's decay. Covid has printed the understanding that we must simply seek to survive the day but attempt to survive the devastation caused by man. The fear of death outweighs our selfish act and must produce a better outcome for Britain. Here, the adoption of universal aims is needed to strengthen Britain during and after Covid.

We must not simply fight against covid, but we must simultaneously fight against the evil within (ourselves). As we have established, man's recklessness has resulted in the prevalence of covid-19. Ultimately our behaviour must change. A connection between the mind-body and soul is needed for the journey ahead; by enhancing the kindness of our souls and inner spirits, we can eradicate our selfish acts and establish universal aims. Evil and greed have no place in our society, and our society must embrace the new age, an age where goodness and goodwill permeate the fibre of our society; regulating our behaviour is the path to the attainment of patriotism, morality, and freedom.

Chapter 24

The Inner Self and the Mask

T HERE IS A LIMIT to our personalities and how they manifest in everyone. Each person in our society has developed a mask covering their true nature. As society dictates our behaviour and preferences, the limits forged by social norms create the necessity for each person to wear a mask. The Mask forms a shield protecting our true selves from internal and external voices. Here, the radio, television, and public voice represent the external voice. The internal voice consists of the voice emanating from our minds. The voice is dissatisfied with our present conditions. The individual wears two types of masks, the first covers the ego, and the second covers the persisting dominance of the ultra-ego. The shame of one's true self and lack of confidence necessitates wearing a mask. Fear of oneself or one's true personality triggers his need to wear a mask, a covering protecting himself from himself. Thus, the mask becomes a representation for legitimising fabricated behaviour. The process generates stress in the person's personality as they cannot exhibit the extent of their true self. The individual develops two moods. Each mood represents a mask, the first and the second Mask. With the development of these moods, individuals attempt to delineate their role in society. The fear of judgment and social disposition becomes a sharp knife hacking into the individual's mind. The wearing of the Mask causes the development of multiple personalities. One that is without ills, the personality that unveils itself in secrecy.

The conflict between the ego and the ultra-ego escalates in the individual's mind in their privacy. In our privacy, we can confirm our identity. However, this identity can only exist under the mould of the Mask. The desired subject shows his need to expose the personality under the Mask. The act of a man dressing up in stockings and high heels expresses his intense interest in his body. In the same instance, a man dressed up in stockings and heels lusting over himself in the mirror represents the adverse effect of social norms—exposing one's hidden self to one's self. Lack of recognition creates an unstable personality seeking acknowledgement and admiration in itself.

Each personality flourishes from recognition. Compliments attain by the ultra-ego provide the person with confidence. However, as the Mask covers the individual's identity, the hidden personality will lack the complement needed to develop confidence. Here, we experience the conflict between the first and second masks, seeking dominance and recognition. An attempt is then made to integrate both masks. This is followed by a further integration with the identity exposed to the public. The personality attempt to remedy these issues leads to the recognition of self. The true self, but the mould of the mast conceals this self. The Mask's concealment of the true self is like a prisoner exploring an avenue to escape from their cell. Yet as this might be impossible, the personalities emerging in one Mask bring oneself internally and externally beyond self-satisfaction. The individual expresses their intense interest in their body and self as much as the public will recognise it. In the act, a self-image is created and regulated by the inner self, scared to expose their true personality. This intensifies one's interest in oneself. They are developing a selfish personality that seeks gratification and ignores the rights of others as they have been ignored by society.

Admiration is necessary; however, the question emerges when it produces selfishness and a narcissistic personality. Then it is recognised that the Mask covering the personality has ceased to exist; the stress experience under the Mask, which has escaped its prison, produced the narcissist personality that is free from judgment and seeks to obtain compliments and recognition in public. The interest in oneself or body overshadows the fabricated personality developed to appease society and adhere to social norms. So is the state of our current existence. Each person battles with themselves to expose their true personality, and each person battles with their internal and external personality for recognition for the ignored personality; the effect contributes to stress and a displease in oneself and their existence in society. Individuals may perceive themselves as not wanted by society as they cannot expose the characteristics of their true selves. The solution is to forgo norms that affect the individual's existence. The individual must and should reveal their true self. If a man wishes to dress up in stockings and heels, so should be the case, and such a personality deserves recognition and admiration from the public; the same applies to a woman seeking the embodiment of a man. The effect will eliminate stress, which is a cause of mental illness, and displease in oneself.

— Chapter 25 —

Mother Africa

Mother Africa, I hear your cry. Mother Africa,
I feel your pain.

Mother Africa, I see your struggles.

Mother of our civilisation, mother of humanity.

I feel your plight. Mother Africa,

I see tears dripping down your face, tears of sorrow,

Through the pain you have harboured for over 500 years.

Mother Africa, your sons, are dying; Mother Africa,
your children are starving.

Mother Africa, your resources are being pillaged.

Your lands have been stolen, Mother Africa; your lands
have been poisoned.

Your children are consumed by hate; your pain
consumes them.

Mother Africa, your children and your lands
are plagued with diseases.

Mother Africa, we have forgotten the lessons of the past,

Mother Africa, we have lost the way of our ancestors.

We have forgotten your teachings.

The teachings kept us solid and pure before
the foreign invasions.

Mother Africa, it is said that you are a scar on the planet.

But you are a warrior in the eyes of your enemies.

Mother Africa, I see you are lonely; I see you are weeping.

Your tears drip and drench your garments; your tears are the
blood of your children,

The blood of those unable to survive starvation,
hunger, slavery,

colonisation, civil wars, wars, and corruption.

The blood of those who persevered to save your children.

Mother Africa, I hear your cry; your tears touch my heart.

Mother Africa, forgive me for my weakness.

Time after time, I tell myself a lie that it will all go away.

Forgive me for hiding from the struggles
facing your children.

Mother Africa, I am weak; I have lost my connection with
the earth and our traditions.

I tremble at the sound of your enemies, mother Africa;
I am weak.

Mother Africa, show me courage; Mother Africa, show
me the way to save your children,

Mother Africa, keep my heart warm,

Mother Africa, show me the way, oh, Mother Africa.

· Chapter 26

The Spirit

M AN'S QUEST FOR THE creation of a utopian society has af-
fected the existence of the soul, and it has created a falsified
existence; such an existence has manipulated the soul and the spirit
to accept the simplification of the world we live in. We have devoted
our lives, mind, and eye to the wonders man has created. The bright
light and the false artificial beauty have leaped the actual and super-
ficial spirits, with a lack of connection with nature. We live in a state
of ignorance, and our material existence enforces perceived free-
dom. Our comprehension of freedom is reckless and thoughtless.
It lacks natural substance; it lacks a connection to the spirit. Today
we live in the solidification of true ignorance. We have exchanged
our objective foundation, a foundation with a connection with the
spirit. We replace our foundation with an artificial existence with a
false understanding of the spirit.

A non-existing spirit is enjoyed through our value of mate-
rial wealth; there is uncertainty in our existence as people. The
will to know the spirit or connect with the spirit is lost. The power
of the will is weakened, and the will's foundation and connection
with the spirit are ignored as our eyes seek a false truth. This false
truth has affected our judgement and truthfulness, endangering
the survival of the spirit.

The mention of the spirit in the context regards our inner-
most being. The true human is born into the world of truth and
has a connection with nature. The spirit, connecting the conscious
life, is the core principle that directs the human mind. The spirit is
the connection between the body, the soul, nature, and truth. The

spirit manifests itself in the connection of humans, a genuine connection outside of material consumption—the awakening of the soul in realising its purpose. The spirit exists outside of the body and lives as a part of the soul or mind. The spirit is the unpolluted blood that flows throughout our veins. The spirit is free of lies and promotes truth. The spirit is the true object of freedom.

Decades of our acceptance of this falsified world have affected our ability to differentiate between what is true and false. Our object today is to maintain seriousness, become the best out of the many, and seek recognition for our actions. In such action, we seek knowledge of the material world. Knowledge is designed to solidify and prolong the existence of the artificial world. In this, we find the embracement of lies and pretends (We lie to take from the poor and acquire articles of no purpose to the spirit and the soul). Money has become our true purpose. With this objective, you ruin the innocence of the spirit, and we ruin the fine and pure virtue of the consciousness. Pursuing material wealth produces the danger of aggression, falsehood, viciousness, suspicion, and pretences. We endanger our souls in our effort to acquire luxury. The man detached from the spirit may find wealth, but with wealth, there is increased stress, enjoying life is limited, and it has replaced with prolonged health issues. Here is the effect of the breakdown of the spirit and the soul.

There is great difficulty in connecting with the spirit. The world we live in poisons the soul and our true purpose in life. The world we live in teaches survival, but not the survival of the soul or the maintenance of the spirit; it teaches the destruction of humanity. It teaches one to wage war to achieve a personal purpose. The artificial world creates a person who is most afraid of himself. He is unsure of the world he lives in. He sleeps little as he fears retribution from his past action. He is consumed by a long-wage war that he can never win, a war that deteriorates the body, mind, soul, and spirit. His survival requires keeping an eye on his enemies; in turn, he dangers the spirit and creates darkness in his heart and soul. His spirit, born white and pure, becomes dark and is consumed by fear of himself. Such fear impacts the soul's ability to leave the body, connect with nature and realise the purpose of his being. His preservation of this wealth makes him an outcast of society. He becomes an outcast not by the people's will but through fear of his undiscovered self. Fear of knowing his purpose and acknowledging what is real, vengeance becomes his purpose, and he is detached from the spirit through this purpose.

To revive the spirit, one should connect with the original foundation of man. That is a connection with nature. That is a connection with people—the understanding of supporting each other and preserving that which is pure and true. The protection of TRUTH becomes paramount. The protection of truth forms the spirit of our survival. The truth saves the spirit and the soul; the truth in its purest form sees no evil and, as such, will set man free from evil. Choosing a good attitude and relationship with man and nature offered the strengthening of the spirit and the attainment of the high spirit. The high spirit softens the heart and gives a sense of real purpose—an understanding of your purpose in life. In saving the spirit, one gains the ability to connect with the outer world. The world is hidden from the naked eye. A world free of materialism and that which commands truth. A man willing to achieve a high spirit should self-sacrifice; through self-sacrifice, he will bring to light that this action has darkened. He will once again connect with nature. He will be recognised not by his wealth but through the brightness of his spirit. He will understand the dangers of selfishness. He will discover the true meaning of human survival. He will have enemies but will be free from his enemies. The strength in the spirit forms his protection. Such a person opened to the higher spirit will be free from ill health. These actions shall and must only exist outside of the material world. They should only exist in the person's true will to connect with the foundation. This action gives man the ability and will to stay true and good to himself.

--------- Chapter 27 ---------

Beautification of Humanity

T HE BEAUTIFICATION OF HUMANITY has contributed to the destruction of humanity; the beautification of humanity has resulted in the artificial human; the beautification of humanity is the cause of the superficial human. People seek flight of their true being when they need to preserve their designed images. Today, we see people (celebrities, the rich man, the so-called online influencers) indulging in their passion for recognition that eluded them from their true forms—the deception of one's true nature. Undoubtedly, the person who exists outside his true form will find emptiness. Such a person is merely scratching the surface of reality, and this person will one day find the need to reach deep into the surface they exist to understand the devastating result of their actions. Self-absorbedness threatens the natural beautification of the person, and we are all born with natural beauty. Even those ousted by society. Those born with mental and physical impairment. In the eye of a man who understands nature's beauty, such a man understands and sees beauty in those deemed unfit by society. Compared to those who, in their determination, have cultivated false images, the impaired person poses the true form of beauty. Those who cultivate false images are self-harming. They experience prolonged revenge against themselves. They experience pain, pain devised by themselves.

We infer how they have destroyed life for themselves in their quest. The extent to which their inner self deteriorates. In the long term, their false image becomes an accurate representation of themselves. A diluted distortion makes the brain believe that that which is false becomes actual, the beautification of nature. The struggle between reality and a deluded mental struggle ensues. False preconceptions affect the person's ability to understand the extent of the damage caused to themselves. For instance, a person admitting to surgery as a means for beautification destroys their natural beauty.

It perhaps influences the psychological issues experienced by the individual. Psychologically, cultivating a false image may permeate the need for recognition or emptiness that the person can address by cultivating a new image. In reality, the new image becomes abstract, and it brings no purpose to address any emptiness felt by the person. Self-pity becomes the existence of the person. This person may appear flourishing to the public, but internally, this person is broken. The assumed flourishing of the person eliminated any notion that this person was seeking assistance. There is a continuous cry for help, which is missed or unheard. The issue results from the false representation which is emitted to society. To love oneself is not to forsake nature, but to destroy oneself for vanity is indeed the destruction of nature.

Chapter 28

Globalisation and Africa

I N MANY WAYS, THE world is moving backwards. Corporations and the media have presented dangerous risks to Africa's ancient culture and traditions. The eradication of African culture has activated nationalism on the continent. Nationalism is a doctrine which was very prominent in the nineteenth century. The central concept of the ideology was based on culture, myths, religion, and indigenous tradition. In Africa today, there is urgent to protect local cultures from foreign influences. The re-enforcement of nationalism means reinstating the old traditions of Africa. Globalisation has brought about integration and migration. Foreign influence has penetrated the existing culture of Africa as the world accelerates towards integration.

The eradication of African culture by foreign influences has contributed to Africa's ongoing development crisis. Although this is the case, we cannot eliminate historical events that also contributed to eradicating the African language. As Nkrumah said, colonial rule removed the old African culture and practices and replaced them with European civilisation. Introducing new cultures has had a detrimental effect on the culture of Africa. The cultural transition from a pre-capitalist society to a capitalist democratic Africa has severely affected African societies. Culture is vital on the African continent as it is employed to organise society. Therefore, the western civilisation imposed by the media from the bottom up has radically transformed the culture of Africa, with adverse effects.

Globalisation is creating a more stable world with economic prosperity for all people. The media presents western society as a model of modern civilisation, which creates the buying society the West depends on. Also, the media is to blame for the various conflicts and wars in developing countries. The media forms the corporations, be it a liberal or conservative majority. Indeed, there are no differences between the media as a corporation and other multinational corporations. However, there are distinctive differences between the media and other corporations. In both cases, the media and corporations sell products on the global market. Yet the product sold by the media is to the people of Africa. The corporation explores the African market. The media aims to serve the interest of powerful western nations. The media serve as a tool in transforming African society into a buying class society for corporations. The media manipulate information or create an illusion that a materialistic world brings happiness and development.

Western media is an essential instrument in the global agenda. The media propagate people to see society as equal and prosperous. The role of the media in Third World societies is to enforce democracy. In addition, the media assist corporations, and the United States (including other powerful nations) in creating the perception that people cannot be trusted to make the right decisions; therefore, power is reserved for those elitists who are perceived as intellectual. Indeed, this is an illusion and false. CNN news has come to replace the ruling elite of Africa and serve as decision-makers for the continent.

Globalisation has harmed Africa's economic and political development. Globalisation has also contributed to the eradication of the indigenous African languages. The British, French, and Portuguese colonialism, democracy and institutions eradicated local dialects in Africa. Modernity and the media have enforced foreign languages on African societies.

Historic globalisation is affecting Africa's development. Historic globalisation (colonialism) has paved the way for modernity and multinational corporations to enforce the western language in Africa. Pressure from multinational corporations and aid donors on African leaders to introduce democracy has weakened the indigenous African language. A bid to open capital-led market economies, which is globalisation, has made it possible for the European language to retain itself in Africa. There are other issues of globalisation which affect several languages. The English language is at the heart of the global process—globalisation is a step towards a globalised language. The education institutions set up during the colonial period also contributed to the disintegration of the African language. The constitution of developing countries is set to have English as their primary communication language. This means the replacement of the local language with English.

—————— Chapter 29 ——————

Corporate power and Ghana's Development

U NDERSTANDING THE THEORY AND ideology behind the for-
mation of corporations gives a good insight into corporate
power. Globalisation is led by the power of multinational corpo-
rations. Corporations have good and bad effects on the lives of the
masses. Corporations are leading the process of globalisation, not
the nation-state, also indicating the decline of the nation-state.
In the era of globalisation, marginalised countries such as Ghana
have become angry about the motives of multinational corpora-
tions. Corporate-led globalisation has brought about poverty and
environmental degradation. Corporations are no new phenom-
enon; they have existed since the sixteenth century in countries
such as Britain and Holland. Corporations go hand in hand with
globalisation. Corporations do not operate to benefit the popula-
tion, but indeed corporations benefit the minority ruling elite and
western power. Abraham Lincoln stated what he saw as an effect
of corporations, *"I see in the near future a crisis approaching that
unnerves me and causes me to tremble for the safety of my country
. . . . Corporations have been enthroned and an era of corruption in
high places will follow"* (Shaw, 1950).

This was the case in Ghana when the government attempted
to solve Ghana's economic crisis, and political instability opened its
door to Multinational Corporations in the 1980s. This later led to
a lack of development in various sectors of the country. Although
Lincoln made this statement in the nineteenth century, this has
since manifested in today's political economy: the United States

and its corporations have become wealthier than the rest of the world. The rise of corporations means corporations will govern the world market and interfere with trade and price control. American-backed corporations control the global market, and globalisation is a corporate-led ideology. American-style capitalism is shaped similarly to Lenin and Trotsky's Bolshevism. Hitler and Mussolini's fascism also forms part of American capitalism.

The authoritarian nature of corporations is established through harsh structural adjustment programmes imposed by corporations through W.T.O. and I.M.F. Not only free trade agreements which do not benefit weak countries such as Ghana. Nigeria is far more stable than Ghana. The Nigerian economy has developed, but corporate-led globalisation is visible in tribal wars, religious conflicts, the increased gap between the wealthy and the poor and high-level corruption.

The intensity of interaction between continents, followed by rapid technological advancement, has made it possible for companies to relocate from one country to another. Corporations trading in Africa and part of the developing South can govern the host nations. When companies find local government policies unfavourable, they move to more favourable countries. Brazil experienced this issue when the socialists won an election victory under Lola.

The I.M.F. resection on Ghana means deregulation; deregulation has led to corporations exploiting the country's resources, environmental degradation, and work hazards. Corporations are enforcers of global democracy, but in reality, corporations represent imperialism and authoritarianism; corporations are based on uneven economic distribution. A corporation enforcing democracy in a country such as Ghana has led to high levels of corruption; this effect of corporate enforcement of democracy was noticed during the period of political instability in Ghana from 1970 to 1995.

Corporate influence has reached all parts of Ghanaian society. Corporations can control the mind of the Ghanaian population using the media as a tool (CNN). We may argue that corporate influence in Ghanaian society has created a consumer-based society;

this, in turn, creates a buying class in Ghanaian society. Because Ghana lacks the economic power of multinational corporations, it enables Transnational Corporations (T.N.C.) to influence public policy and government policy. Corporate influence ranges from the financing of elections and the creation of think tanks. They influence the political blocks in Ghana and other African states.

Globalisation is being led by corporations. Multinational corporations' wealth allows them to influence countries through globalisation. Deregulation has allowed corporations to benefit, but this is at the cost of people in many nations. Deregulation and corporate power mean less economic benefit to Ghana, environmental deregulation, high levels of corruption etc. Corporate influence in Ghana, as Nkrumah explained, means neo-colonialism and imperialism. Corporate power can also be viewed as the free market, democracy, economics, and power. There is no significant proof to indicate the eradication of the nation-state by the multinational, but then we can argue that economic power has assisted corporations in becoming more influential.

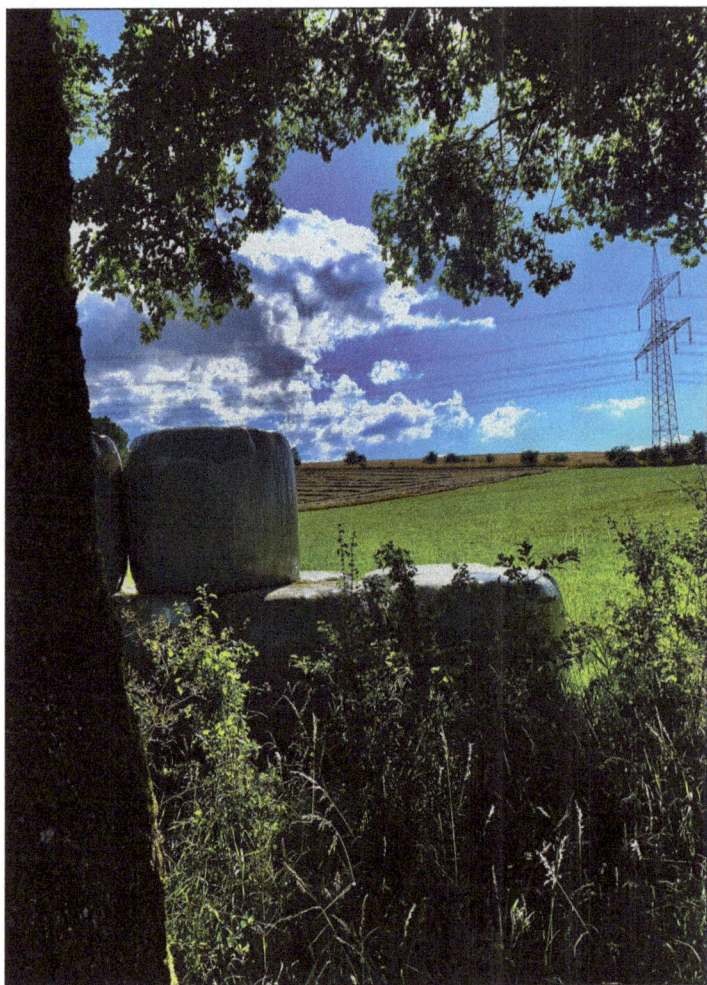

Chapter 30

Africa and the rest of the world

T HE ATROCITIES OF 9/11 and the war in Afghanistan and Iraq have raised questions about the dominance of the U.S.A. The war on terror was the self-preservation of the United States. The United States government uses American forces backed by the pentagon to attack and contain its competitors. Terrorism has become an effective mechanism used by the United States and its Allies for their continuous invasions. Today we are witnessing a shift from the threat of communism to Islamic terror. I believe this justifies the Americans to create global police, which will help enable their goal to achieve total domination. For the United States to maintain its hegemony, the government had to create trepidation in public. This fear made it easy to spread neoliberalism and American capitalism, which the U.S. claims will bring about economic equality. Indeed, the policies adopted by the United States will further the stagnation in the Continent of Africa and other developing countries.

With bilateral police, the world will be dominated by a western hegemonic force which will repress the rest of the world. We are again observing a possible decline of a superpower. Possibly, we are witnessing the rise of China as a global power. The bipolar management of the world has emerged. The decline of the United States is no fault of its government or the population, but it is a natural process. History has witnessed the rise of many empires; similarly, empires are born to rise and decline. With the United States, the question is, are they ready to accept their decline? It is without a doubt that a declining state will attempt to hold onto its power. The process will require a change of political ideology or the forging of alliances, which will ensure growth. Perhaps, the United States will re-identify itself as a peace broker, not global police, or defender of democracy.

Chinese growth and its rapid development are a threat not only to the United States but to the West. We discount Russia, as it is evident that the Russian government persist in maintaining its position as a threat or enemy to the West. This is featured in the current war in Ukraine. The war in Ukraine has amplified the west fear of its decline. The imposing of sanctions on Russia and its friends sets an example. As a British citizen living in London. I have observed that the sanction imposed by our government is detrimental to the U.K., perhaps to the Russian government. We are currently experiencing a rise in food and fuel prices. Poverty is on the increase in the country. Yet, the United Kingdom maintains a position which is detrimental to itself. As an ally to the United States, perhaps the decline of the U.S. will spell out the further decline of Great Britain.

Britain needs to re-examine its partnership and relationships with the World (Africa and the developing South). The African is a scar on the planet. He lays at the bottom of the race structure. His dark skin is his weakness in every part of the world; he is underestimated and degraded. However, as much as it is a scar on the planet, tomorrow, it will emerge as a global superpower. The African is said to be ineffective, foolish, and unable to govern himself. However, the world is ignorant, and the notion that Africa will remain the poorest continent is erroneous.

Then again, Africa needs to put its house in order. There is a need for strategic development plans which will ensure its emergence as a superpower. African leaders should focus on developing their countries per their culture. The introduction of western ideology is harmful to our development. Africa should call for a second wave of African independence. The second wave of African independence should encompass political, social, and economic independence (Total freedom from its colonial masters). Africa should focus on outward trade, integrate its markets, and protect them. Self-preservation is essential for its development. The fall of a superpower is an opportunity for the rise of a developing state. Thus, Africans should prepare to understand their future relationship with the world. Africa should refrain from seeking loans and aid, act responsibly, and focus on devising policies that will ensure its ability to embrace future opportunities. The changes on the global stage are eminent and an opportunity for Africa. The emerging African empire will focus on promoting world peace; our plight in the past will set the precedence and dictate our behaviour toward the rest of the world. Peace and no war are the focus of the Africans. Yet, there is a need to strengthen our military capability. Africa's survival depends on its ability to embrace its forgotten cultures and tradition. This tradition is the strength of the Africans. Western ideology belongs to the West and the African tradition, and its native language belongs to the African.

The question concerns understanding the continent's ability to emerge as a superpower. One may argue that this is a dream as Africa is divided by languages and different cultures. There are two ways Africa can Unite; Unification can be forced through war. War will effectively break down the borders and barriers developed by the Europeans. On the other hand, a negotiated unification process is possible. The United States emerged as a superpower because of the civil war and the Second World War. The creation of a permanent armed economy, enforced by the United States of Africa, is necessary for an African superpower's survival. America's national interest policy indicates a defensive and offensive policy. This is prominent in Bush's Doctrine of pre-emptive war stated in the United States National Security Council and entitled National Security Strategy of the United States, published in 2002. The spread of Neoconservatism abroad also indicates what Trotskyists identify as a permanent revolution.

Chapter 31

Praying with Light and Water

G ROWTH IS ESSENTIAL IN our lives. People experience different forms of growth in life: spiritual growth, mental growth, occupational growth, and growth in their faith. Growth is an evolution comprising a string of changes and development. It encompasses a process in which simple things eventually become complex. When you observe growth in yourself, you will understand that when growth is successful, it is accompanied by joy and happiness; when growth fails, people experience levels of pain and depression. Man seeks to ensure growth in every aspect of life; however, as there is inconsistency in growth and a lack of continuity, man must search for a higher purpose that, outside of growth, can provide him with the needed stimulation. That is a positive stimulation outside of pain and depression. Some believe that the church may offer such stimulation. In others, the needed stimulation is found in material consumption. Material consumption replaces emptiness.

My understanding of life is that it is full of complexity. Complexity makes life what it is and understanding this complexity should offer one the satisfaction needed to grow. Life without the complexity and continuous happiness will eventually contrive unhappiness in the person as such nature has offered a balance in its effort to afford man growth. The balance is present in happiness and pain. There is an intertwined relationship between happiness and pain; the relationship between happiness and pain promotes motivation in a person. It is a natural stimulus, encouraging the pursuit of growth in every person.

I recommend different types of stimuli that can provide happiness to each person. Here, I refer to the act of prayer. We all pray, and we all pray to a supreme being whom we believe has the answers to our struggles. Some pray through Jesus, others through idols, animals, and other entities. We believe the supreme being offered us protection, and he designed our destiny. These are no falsified assumptions. People from different faiths can testify that through prayer, they experience changes in their lives. Although blessed with the means to afford material articles, the wealthy man prays for long life, health, and the ability to maintain happiness. It is evident that although wealthy, happiness cannot be discovered in money. In fact, with money comes the potential to be unhappy. In the poor man, prayer comprises the need for wealth and happiness. The poor man has little to live on; however, compared with the rich person, he is happier. Nevertheless, the rich and the poor have dissatisfaction, unhappiness, and regrets. I find prayer as the remedy in these situations.

I contest that all men should engage in prayer. There are methods which I find helpful. I find that through this method, the answer to my prayers is immediate. Pray using water and light. When used in prayer, water and light are essential elements transporting messages from our world to the spirit world. Water is life, and light is illumination; with light, one's mind is open to understanding the unknown.

If you require an immediate answer to your prayers, I recommend praying in the early morning. I recommend praying around 3 am; the significance of this time is that the earth will be vibrating. The earth's vibration is good for the soul and the body. The hour stipulated is peaceful as the world is at rest; the communication channels between the spiritual worlds are open and promote the free flow of information. You should always pray on your knees, showing you are humble and accepting that there is a supreme force controlling every aspect of life. You should pray, acknowledging that you are just a man, but then understanding that God has a purpose for you, and through prayer, you are submitting yourself to receive your purpose. This prayer should be performed outside your home, perhaps in the garden.

Alternatively, when praying indoors, pray in the morning; before praying, attempt to meditate for 15 minutes. Meditate by opening your curtains. Invite light into your room when meditating. Meditate while sitting on the floor or on a chair. After meditation, get on your knees with your head facing the light. Submit yourself to the supreme being by recognising this power during this time. For example, you can utter the words, God, I submit myself to you. I recognise that I am on this earth to serve your purpose. You can ask for forgiveness. Ensure that when praying, your request is clear and precise. Be clear about your request and explain its purpose and importance to your outer and inner growth as a person.

Water is a powerful substance and should be used in prayer. There is a method you should subscribe to when using water during prayer. After praying, ensure you pour water three times onto the ground. You should pray when taking a bath, and this is highly recommended. After cleaning yourself into a clear and purest form, you should pray in the shower. You can pray when you stay in a pool of water.

On the other hand, praying by a river or at the beach is also effective. At the beach, you will find that all the positive spirits, including angels, are assembled, ready to listen and support you in your prayer. The same will manifest when you pray at the river. Use clean and clear water to pray at the river and the beach. After praying, pour the water into the river or the sea.

In my experience, you will see an answer to your prayer within no more than two days when you employ the method described. It is essential to understand that the most effective measure, when faced with uncertainty in life, is to pray.

HUMAN
RIGHTS

—— Chapter 32 ——

The Humble Man

I AM HUMBLE. YES, I am humble
I live a righteous life and am humble; I fear no man, as I am humble; God, the gods, and the supreme beings are my protectors. I am humble. I am humble; I do not steal nor take from no one. I am humble. I am humble and live a peaceful life; forgiveness is my strength and not my weakness; I am free from my enemies, those who seek to harm me, and those to defame my character. I am humble. I have no desire for trouble, I am free from trouble, I live within my means, and I am blind to the evil man do. I am humble. I pray that all men will be free from themselves and their wickedness one day. Free from the jaws of the system and free from their self-destruction.

I pray that all men will identify as men; I am humble, I dream of a world without race, I dream of a world without division, I am humble. I am a man of all faith and a lover of all creatures. No matter the situation, I preserve my dignity. I disengage from my ego, my superego, and the ultra-ego. I am humble. I feed from the land, and I am one with the land; I take what I need from the land, and my joy is in preserving the land. I find friendship in those who believe in the simple things in life. In the passion of life, I seek not to destroy humanity but to save humanity from himself. I am humble. I am humble because it makes me pure. I am intertwined with the earth, fire, water, and the wind, which are the element and source of my protection. These elements are pivotal to my survival. I am humble, and I am free from those who seek my demise, I am free from those who wish my downfall, I am the man who is gifted by nature, I am humble, I am free from stress and free from diseases, I walk with my head held high, I am humble.

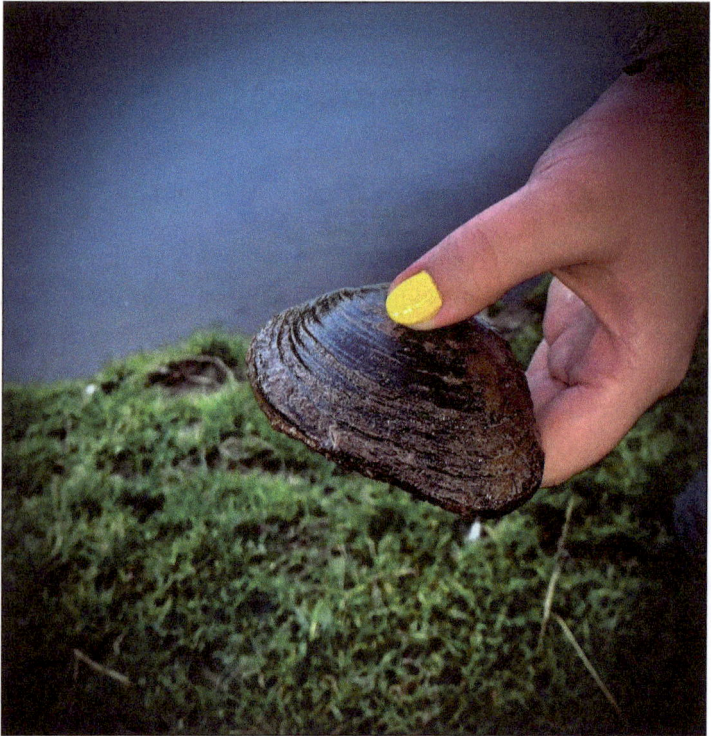

—— Chapter 33 ——

Speaking to Death

Y ESTERDAY YOU SAID GOODBYE, and I watched you cry; you said you missed me and would miss me. Yesterday, I saw you cry, and you said I was a perfect human being; you said I was your friend. Yesterday, I watched you cry, and you asked why I was gone and why I did not say goodbye. Yesterday I watched you cry; you said you could not live without me; life would be meaningless without me. Yesterday, I saw you in the company of my friends and enemies, and you were with those who gained from my death; you are with those who will suffer after my death. Yesterday you buried me, cremated me, spread my ashes over the sea, and placed my ashes in an urn beside your bed.

You were at my grave yesterday, laid down flowers, cried, and remembered our favourite locations. Yesterday you spoke about how we used to dance. You talk about where we ate, and the good times we had together.

You have forgotten the troubles that divided us; you ask why I left you, you wondered why I left so early, you wondered why I had to go, yesterday, you said you forgive me, you forgive me for leaving you so soon, you forgive me for cheating on you, you are forgiven for spending all our saving, you said you understood that life is worth more than money. You said the money could not replace the good time we had. You said you forgave me for the argument. Yesterday whilst at my grave, you called me daddy, you called me mother, you called me sister, you called me brother, you called me your cousin. Yesterday at my grave, you called me grandmother, you called me grandfather, you called me your friend, and you called me your lover.

It was yesterday when I jumped from the 25th floor, and it was yesterday when I was pushed off the 25th floor. It was yesterday when I shot myself. It was yesterday when I hung myself. It was yesterday when that man raped and killed me, and yesterday my mother killed me. My brother stabbed me, and I died during the shelling of Iraq by the Americans. I died during a roadside bombing in Afghanistan; I died from starvation in Africa. I died during the Zulu wars. I died during the Ashanti wars. Yesterday, I died when fighting in the Napoleonic wars. I died in a German gas chamber, and I died in your arms.

I hear you cry and your words; you called me the dead and the departed. You called me the deceased. And you called me the one who passed away. You said I was no more; I have passed to the other world—the world of the unknown. You said I am no more with the living, but I am alive, without my body, without the vessel that provides you with a visual representation of me, but I am with you. I am dead, but I live. I sit beside your bed when you sleep and walk with you on the street; I hold your hand when you cry, shouting you miss me. I am the whispers in your ear; I am the voices you refuse to acknowledge.

Yesterday, I was dead, but today I live. I live in a land free of human laws, but in this land, there are laws. I am free from all human limitations, social norms, and financial restrictions that limited my existence when I was in my vessel. I walk this earth as much as you do. I have friends. I have developed a new relationship in the new land. In the beginning, I was confused. I walked the spirit world for two weeks before acknowledging I was without my body.

I died a poor man, so in this land, I am poor. I passed a rich man, so in this world, I am rich. While with the living, I said, money does not matter; it matters in this life. Today in my temporary transition, particular articles are essential. I am far from entering into the light, as in my past life, I was a thief. Today, I am far from entering the light as I stole from the poor in my past life. I was a liar; I killed. In this life, I will need prayer from a man with a pure heart to transition into the light. Today I regret my past. Today, I am in purgatory, as I have committed suicide. Today I am in purgatory as I was murdered. I will walk this land until my murderer is punished and live in purgatory until my revenge is complete. I will need a confession from my killer to transition into the next life. Yet there is a next life, that life I am told is full of happiness. Only those who confess their sins can enter this life. Yet I will need a man with a pure heart to pray for my transition. My riches are wealthless in the next life.

While living with the undead, I was consumed with material consumption. I ignored the need for spirituality. I forgot the rituals of my ancestors. I thought I was wise, and I thought money was the answer. I felt a new car, and a house would be fulfilling. But today, I suffer, as the forgotten rituals of my ancestors are needed for me to ascend towards the light. The land of the dead is the first step from the afterlife. Although I am free, my past life of wickedness has impacted my ability to achieve total freedom.

Today, I pray you will have a happy life, a life from your material consumption. Free yourself from meat, drugs, and alcohol and free yourself from wickedness. Meat expires after seven days. Expired meat is bad for your health and your mental and spiritual development. Eat healthily and live healthily. Engage in the fast; fasting will assist you in purifying your body. Observing the fast will remove poisonous waste from your body. It will open the channel between you and the spirit world. The poison you consume limits your ability to communicate with me. For I am beside you; pray to achieve humbleness; a free soul and a peaceful mind are needed to communicate with me. Today you must activate your mind, and you will understand the dead through this activation. I am dead because you have lost the human capacity to communicate with me. This capability was shared by your ancestors, who were one with nature.

Pay attention to your dreams. I reveal myself in your dream. But to you, it's just a dream. Through your dreams, I can communicate my needs. Through your dreams, I can provide you with answers to your questions and reveal the reasons for your struggles.

The best form of communication is to call my name when you pray. You can employ the ancient method of speaking to the dead. This method requires using pure cow milk. With the milk, you pray as you hold the milk as a microphone. Call my name and say the reason for your communication. Then pour half of the milk into a river, stream, or sea. Before pouring, the remaining have a taste and then pour the remaining milk. Another method for communicating with me is by pouring libation.

Through these methods, I promise to make myself visible in your dream with the answers you seek. Yesterday I was alive, yesterday, I was dead, but today I live I am with you.

---------- Chapter 34 ----------

My Body and My Health

Y OU IGNORE US, YOU ignore our importance to your survival,
you take our lives for granted, and you take me for granted.
You disregard our happiness and your well-being; your ignorance
is your downfall. It is the root of your struggles. But without us,
your existence is meaningless. Without us, you are non-existing,
and your life will be cut short. We are your body and mind. We
appear to be two individuals, but we are one. The body and mind
are like Siamese twins; one does not move without the other. We
have been attached from birth. We are inseparable. One is the
servant of the other, and together our functioning guarantees
your survival. I, the body, respond to requests from the mind;
without the mind, I am not functional.

I observe the deliberate and automatic response from the
mind, and I am calling out for better treatment. I am calling out
for your recognition. Reframe your adverse action. Reframe from
polluting my existence with poison that weakens my survival. I am
your body and mind. By polluting the mind with poison and un-
lawful thoughts, I begin to disintegrate. However, I became strong
with a healthy life and the responses of good thoughts and happi-
ness. My strength is derived from the brain. The brain controls my
ability to maintain my youth and beauty. The root of your disease
and ill health comes from what you eat and say. Your negative
thought is the path to disease and illness. Your negative thoughts
manifest in your action. And they become a quintessential part
of your life. Damaging as they are, they manifest from your cre-
ation, and they manifest from your mind. Your unhealthy lifestyle

emanating from your food, alcohol and drug consumption is a cause of disease that rapidly kills me. The poison you consume travels through your bloodstream and affects my ability to operate. It infects me, paralysing me, affects my ability to send messages to the body, and affects your ability to function in your daily activities effectively. Impure thoughts, stress and anxiety shutter my ability to provide you with strength. They are crippling and unacceptable. They impact my power to ensure your survival. With these, you will frequently visit hospitals and clinics, searching for solutions. Yet you cause these issues. I am your mind and body.

Today I bring to your attention my deepest fear. Today I bring to your attention the damage you have caused. Today I request to admit to changes that will increase your life expectance, change that will allow me to maintain proper functionality. Avoid getting stressed and destroying me but discover and maintain my dominance by admitting to purity in your thought and actions. Through your thought, you create disease. These diseases affect your skin and affect your presence. The disease and poisons flowing through your body develop the wrinkles undesired by you and society. Tomorrow, you will hide from yourself and in drains, searching for your former beauty. You will become a shadow of your one's healthy body. Changes in your diet and thought are warranted to avoid your disintegration. Impress in your mind sound and positive thought that can manifest in good health. A continuous unclean thought is an instrument for disaster, significant damage that will lead to your life's loss. The perfect remedy is an ideal thought. I am your body and mind today.

I impress my wishes and request that you live healthily. You should eat no less than three times a day. Do not eat after 6 pm, and you should maintain cleanliness, cleanliness fosters purity in the mind and body. Attempt to fast for one week every month; the fast will allow cleaning all impurities and diseases from your bloodstream. Eat fresh vegetables and do not eat meat. The plant offers protein and the mineral you will obtain from eating meat. Committing to drinking water regularly during the day, possess health, reframe from wickedness, envy, and greed. Devote yourself to an uplifting life and free yourself from corruption, give unto those who deserve rewards and again be charitable.

—— Chapter 35 ——

What I believe In

I BELIEVE THAT ALL MEN are equal. However, I disregard the concept of race; I think a man should be judged according to his contribution to society and not by the colour of his skin. Race classification is responsible for most of the social displacement being experienced today. I believe that race has set a backward spiral and the unevenness of our society. Equally, I think every man has a right to choose; therefore, he has a right to identify as gay, transgender, or bisexual. His sexuality should not hinder his progression as a person; This notion applies to the development of women. I believe in social integration. Again, I disregard the creation of space in society—for example, the creation of space for women or people with different sexual orientations. The creation of space, in effect, constitutes the separation of one's identity from society. I believe that through social integration, we can all learn to accept and understand our differences.

I believe in religion, and I identify with all faiths. I believe that religious classification is harmful to society. I think that all beliefs negatively and positively influence people and culture. People with extreme religious beliefs should not be isolated but should be offered a platform for self-expression. Providing them with a platform will mitigate the possibility of violent action.

Moreover, it is unjust to classify such individuals as unfit for society. Diverse views are essential to human progression. Through contradiction in ideas, we can develop a new concept that has the propensity for ensuring development.

I believe in the existence of spirit. I think that we humans are not the sole habitat of this planet. I believe that as must as there are good and evil people, equally there are good and bad spirits. Those who are susceptive to the supreme being understand that the supreme being rules over good and evil. Further, there is no evidence to suggest that the supreme being, the creator of the universe, is a male or female. However, when in the company of humans, the supreme being embodied the shape of a man, woman, or child. I believe that both good and evil spirits follow people, and these spirits influence our actions. Some of these influences are vocal, and others are undetected by our ears or eyes. For example, there was a story of a man who could communicate with spirits; his wish was to become rich. One summer, as he walked past a supermarket, he heard a voice; the voice asked him to enter the supermarket; he entered the supermarket and bought three lottery numbers made available to him by the voice. That night he became a millionaire. The same was with a man being followed by a bad spirit; this spirit taught him evil.

As previously mentioned, one can communicate with the spirit through dreams or visions. However, such a person must be disciplined and able to control his mind. It would help if you attempted to understand the symbols revealed to you in your dream. Vision is like a puzzle; it needs attention and dedication to interpret. Different spirit poses different power, and their powers are transferred to the person. For instance, the person may have the power of healing or vision. It is essential to understand that my belief does not attempt to disregard the inherited talent or abilities of the individual. Some individuals are aware of the presence of spirit in their lives. These individuals may wish to detach themselves from the spirit. One should understand that your relationship with the spirit is not permanent. You can choose to maintain the relationship or separate yourself from the spirit. In any case, prayer and readings from the book of psalms can help with such an objective. There are also passages in the Quran that serve the same purpose. However, in most cases, a spirit may demand a ritual before agreeing to detach himself from a person.

We speak to spirits every day. One may argue that humans are a form of spirit. This assertion is correct. However, this chapter focuses on the spirit without human forms. Spirit can appear as human. They have jobs as humans do; they walk and work amongst us. They visit the beach, restaurants, and cinemas; some are married to humans. There are marriages in physical and spiritual forms. Spirits can travel from one realm to the other within minutes. Some live in the ocean, under the earth and in different galaxies. In these universes, there are power struggles. There is a complex political structure. There are also technological advancements that are more advanced than we have today. In their spiritual realm, there are wars. Indeed, spirits are no different to humans; there are religions. Some are Muslim, Christians, Buddhist, and Hindu. Some are more religious than humans and live to serve the interest of the supreme being. These spirits are committed to prayer and pray for a world without wars. They pray for peace. They pray for unity between humans and the spirit. They pray that one day all men and spirits will gather and pray against the evils that exist amongst us.

Using these instructions, you can break the barrier between yourself and the invisible spirit following you. Visit the beach during the day or at night. Bring a bottle of dry gin, a candle, and a bottle of water. Light the candle and pray, then pour libation; whilst pouring libation, vocalise your purpose. After completing this instruction, fetch some seawater. Before you go to bed, wash with the seawater, and allow the water to dry. Within days, you will experience strange dreams. Again, pay attention to your dream, as the spirit will communicate with you. It is essential also to understand that this process can be dangerous to a person being followed by an evil spirit. Seek advice from someone with experience in the field before embarking on these instructions.

Chapter 36

Mental Imaging and My Desire

O UR CURRENT STATE OF mind, in its object, eliminates the vitality of the essence of visualisation. People are today ignorant of their existence. People take for granted the power of the mind. The mind has the power to give what you need. The mind has the power to communicate with the universe and effect changes in the universe which will benefit your personal development. Mental imaging is a powerful practice that can assist individuals in realising their dreams and desires.

The practice of mental imaging is a necessary step to affecting the manifestation of one's dreams and desires. The process, however, encompasses the visualisation of one's thoughts. The process embodies the individual formulating a mental image, and the development is the architect of their wishes or desire, just as in constructing a building. The initial process is the desire to build a house, then the land acquisition; the proceeding stage toward building our desired house is drawing the plan. The architect draws your desired building, demonstrating the house's size and the room's shapes and contours.

Similarly, when concerned with your desires, you must develop a firm plan that is fixed in your mind. The developed image is fixed in your mind, then emits your wishes to the universe and manifests. Some principles and disciplines govern the use of mental images. Visualisation or mental imaging is not a simple task of developing an image; it requires a disciplined mind and the ability to focus on the developed image. Concentration is vital in visualisation, influence, and one's ability to draw on a strong influence between the mind and the universe, producing an accuracy of your desire and wishes. The power of concentration is the force behind mental imaging. A person who desires to buy a car should first create a mental image of the car, including the type of car, the model, the engine type, the colour of its interior, the engine size, and the car's shape. Having developed the image of the car, you should then develop the image of you owning the car. Perhaps an image of you driving the car. By using the power of concentration, impress this vision in your mind and focus on the image. Your concentration should eliminate any negative factors in your thought that may affect the process. The elimination of environmental influences is crucial in this practice. Indeed, through the art of concentration, you can free your mind of all negative thoughts that might affect the manifestation of the desire. Concentration allows the soul to connect with the universe; the communication between the soul, your mind, and the mental image of your need will manifest as your desire.

The creation of mental images is the core function of your life, far from the manifestation of your desires. You practice the application of mental images in your daily activity unconsciously. For instance, a scientist experimenting or an inventor wishing to invent a new device will first develop a mental image of the device before engaging in its production. Also, a person seeking employment in a company will create a mental image of themselves working at the company. Of course, creating a mental image of a successful interview can eventually force the manifestation of your employment at the company. Here, the premise suggests that the conscious and unconscious deployment of mental imaging effect the realisation of one's desire.

The use of mental images must be employed without prejudice. As a strategy, the process depends on the intensity of the connection between the internal and external forces. The time interval between creating the mental image and its manifestation depends on one's desire. The manifestation of one's desire can transpire within days. For instance, if you desire to acquire £10 for an emergency undertaking, the manifestation of such desire may transpire within days.

The manifestation of your mental image depends on the clarity of the image. Also, the time interval between developing your mental image and its manifestation depends on the clarity of the mental image. On the other hand, if one wishes to become president of the country, as this is a significant undertaking, the time interval between mental imaging and the manifestation of your desire is expected to be more significant. The actual manifestation of the mental image and its manifestation is subject to the person having a concrete understanding of what they desire. A better understanding of your desire is a necessary step toward its realisation. Continuous practice of the mental image of the image is required. A persisting practice recalls the image in your memory; the practice influences the desire or the material image manifesting.

─────── Chapter 37 ───────

About Diet and Health

Y OUR DIET IMPACTS THE body and mind. It is common knowl-
edge that the brain requires food to operate. I insist that the
mention of food should not be taken casually. By mentioning food,
I stress the quality of food we consume. I also stress the quantity
of food we consume. I was brought up with the understanding
that quantity supersedes quality. The body needs just enough food
to operate and function properly. Overindulgence in food is un-
healthy as such practices have consequences. People from a humble
beginning in Africa, where most families experienced a financial
issue, see it as a privilege to have food. The food they ate was high
in carbohydrates, with less meat. However, the food is rich in herbs,
providing the body with the necessary nutrients.

The concept of overindulgence in food is the African way; as
pleasurable as it may appear, this process affects individual pro-
ductivity. Overindulgence in food produce fatigue. It impacts the
body to function and thus reduces its productivity. In addition,
overeating is causation for health problems such as obesity, which
is common in most nations. It is essential to understand that the
information I have divulged in this chapter concerns my personal
experience with food. Therefore, my recommendation might not
apply to different body types.

However, in my experience, I have understood that eating less
is healthy for the body. Eating less reduces stress on the stomach
and our digestive system. Also, eating less reduces the possibility of
irritable bowel syndrome. These are my recommendations; I rec-
ommend you drink warm water each morning. The warm water

reduces the acid that develops overnight. I also indulge in drinking warm ginger, lime and honey each morning—this is a mandatory process in my daily activity. In the morning, I reframe from eating a large breakfast. I have fruit or dry toast for breakfast.

In 2021, I engaged in a 40-day fast. After the end of the 40-day fast, I visited the beach to pray. I prayed for 15 minutes, and during my prayer, I observed the presence of an old lady. This woman was around 58 years old. The lady approached me and then engaged in a conversation with me. During our conversation, we spoke about a world without war and the possibility of people existing without hate. While conversing with the woman, I enquired about her age; she then mentioned that she was 80. Her name was Margret; I was astonished at this revelation as I was sure she was in her late 50s. I inquire into the secret of acquiring a youthful look. She said there was no secret, but it was a matter of eating well. She said she drank about 8 cups of water every day. She was free from consuming sugar. She insists that sugar contains poison that affects the quality of one's health. I agreed with her contention as I knew of sugar's adverse health effects. Before my conversation with the woman, I understood that sugar caused diabetes, inflammation, high blood pressure, and other diseases in the body. Margaret said she did not consume meat and was free from using drugs as a preventative measure. I then told Margaret that I take pleasure in consuming meat and that it was difficult to eliminate meat from my diet. At this statement, Margaret looked into my eye and said that I needed to exclude meat from my diet if I wanted to have a long life but be in good health. Since my conversation with Margaret, I have taken her advice and removed the meat from my diet.

I can confess that my skin's texture and complexion have improved significantly. I am stronger and freer from headaches. Before encountering Margaret, I experienced persistent head-aches and fatigue. Today my energy levels are high, and I am more active than previous. I run four times a day, mainly in the evenings. I have taken to boxing and bodybuilding. My confi-dence level has improved, and I have noticed that my work pro-ductivity has increased.

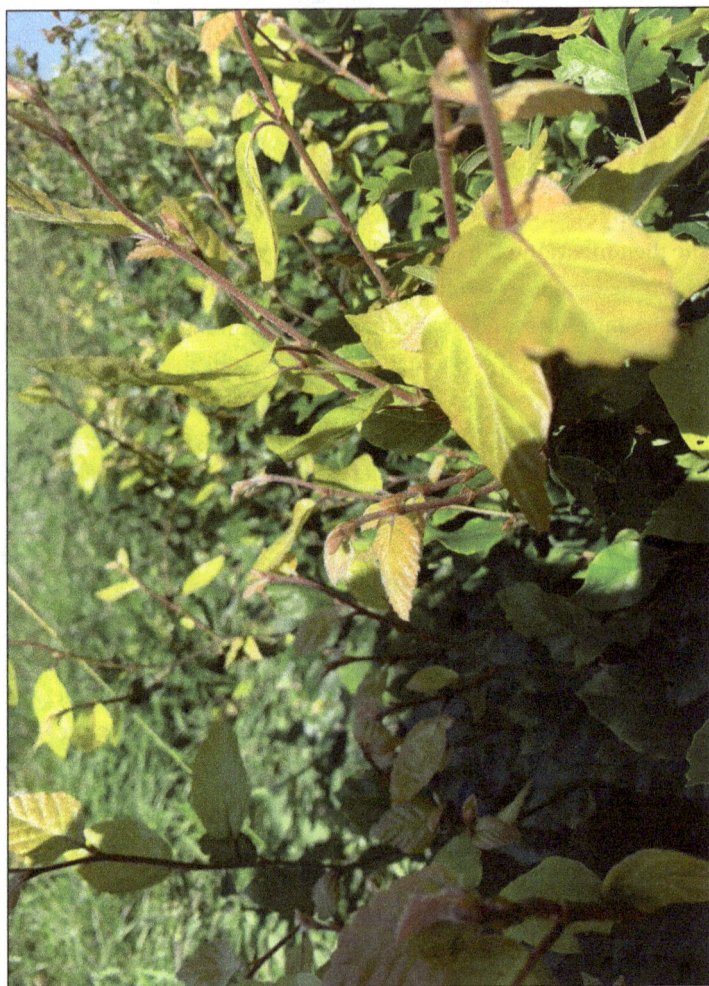

Chapter 38

A message from Air and Water

H UMANS ARE STUPID; WE laugh at you; shame is your name. You maintain your presence as the masters of the universe, but you are simply stupid. You are slaves to your development and progress. You, humans, are stupid; you destroy all that is good in the name of progress. You, humans, are stupid; when would you realise the end is near? Nature is not responsible for your end. Stupid humans, we gave you the air you breathe and the water you drink. 80% of your body mass consists of water, and your existence is fatal; without water or air, you poison your water in the name of progress and development. You poison your water sources through mining activities. You dump toxic waste into your rivers and streams. You produce products dangerous to your health and dump the waste into your source of drinking water.

Humans are stupid. You, humans, have passed the stage of stupidity and are now heading to extinction. Your stupidity is recognisable. You espouse polluting water needed for the cultivation of your food. You pray for long life, but you destroy that which will have the source of life and can guarantee you a long life. Humans are stupid; you pollute the air you breathe and dismiss the understanding that you will be extinct without fresh air. You pollute the air with the awareness of the impact of risks on your existence. You took your first breath from the air; all living organisms require air to survive. But you are blinded by greed and stupidity. You are willing to destroy that which is already perfect for generating wealth. You, humans, are stupid.